For my fantastic sisters, Kiwi and Biddy – R. G.

Barefoot Books, 3 Bow Street, 3rd Floor, Cambridge MA 02138
Illustrations copyright © 2002 by Rachel Griffin. The moral right of Rachel Griffin to be
identified as the illustrator of this work has been asserted. First published in the United States
of America in 2002 by Barefoot Books, Inc. All rights reserved. No part of this book may be
reproduced in any form or by any means, electronic or mechanical, including photocopying,
recording, or by any information storage and retrieval system, without permission in writing from
the publisher. This book was typeset in: Cloister, Snell, Angelo, Fontesque, DellaRobbia, Spring,
HotsyTotsy, Nuptial, Mason, Pepita, Remedy, Democratica, Chophouse, Arrus 24pt.
The illustrations were created with embroidered collage and handmade papers. Graphic design by
Spencer Hawes, England. Color transparencies by Jonathan Fisher Photography, England. Color
separation by Bright Arts Singapore. Printed and bound in China by South China Printing Co.
(1988) Ltd. This book is printed on 100% acid-free paper

1 3 5 7 9 8 6 4 2

Publisher Cataloging-in-Publication Data (U.S.)
Twelve days of Christmas (English folk song).
The twelve days of Christmas / illustrated by Rachel Griffin.-1st ed. [32] p. : col. ill. , cm.
Accompanied by: 1 sound disc : digital, stereo. ; 4 3/4in.
Summary: Each verse of this traditional Christmas carol is accompanied by a spread
of tactile artwork inspired by various cultural traditions.
ISBN 1-84148-940-9
1. Folk songs, English — England —Texts. 2. Christmas music —Texts.
3. Folk songs — England. 4. Christmas music.
I. The twelve days of Christmas. II. Griffin, Rachel.
782.42/ 1723 21 CIP   PZ8.3.T8517 2002

Twelve Days of Christmas

Rachel Griffin

Barefoot Books
Celebrating Art and Story

On the first day of Christmas
My true love gave to me

A partridge in a pear tree.

On the second day of Christmas
My true love gave to me

Two turtle-doves,

And a partridge in a pear tree.

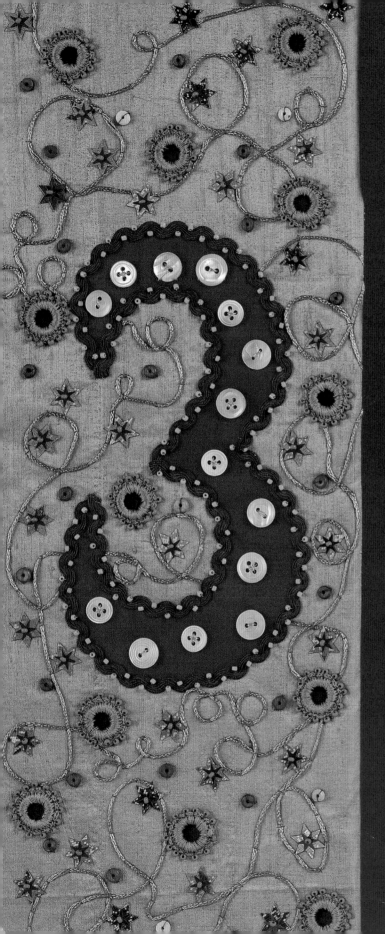

On the third day of Christmas
My true love gave to me

Three French hens,

Two turtle-doves,

And a partridge in a pear tree.

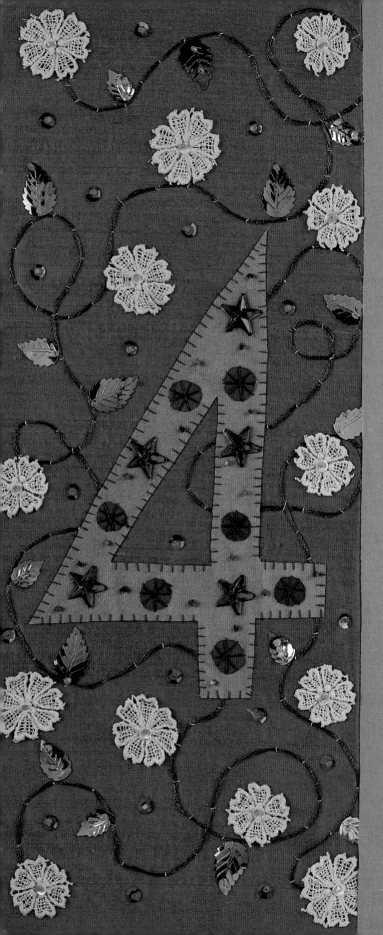

On the fourth day of Christmas
My true love gave to me

Four calling birds,

Three French hens,

Two turtle-doves,

And a partridge in a pear tree.

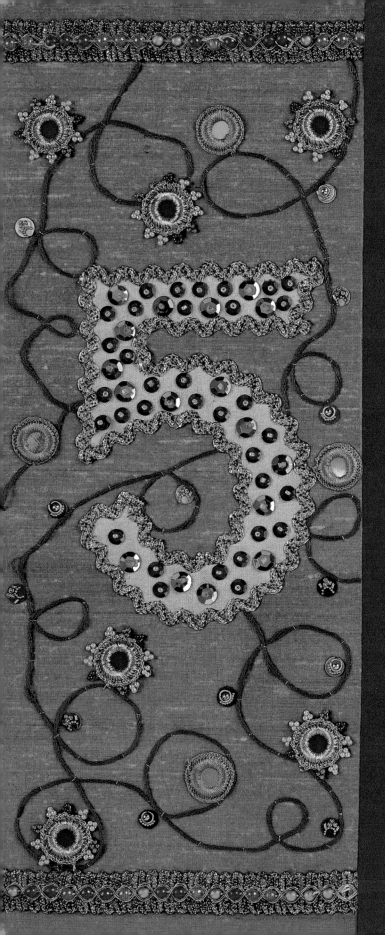

On the fifth day of Christmas
My true love gave to me

Five golden rings,
Four calling birds,
Three French hens,
Two turtle-doves,
And a partridge in a pear tree.

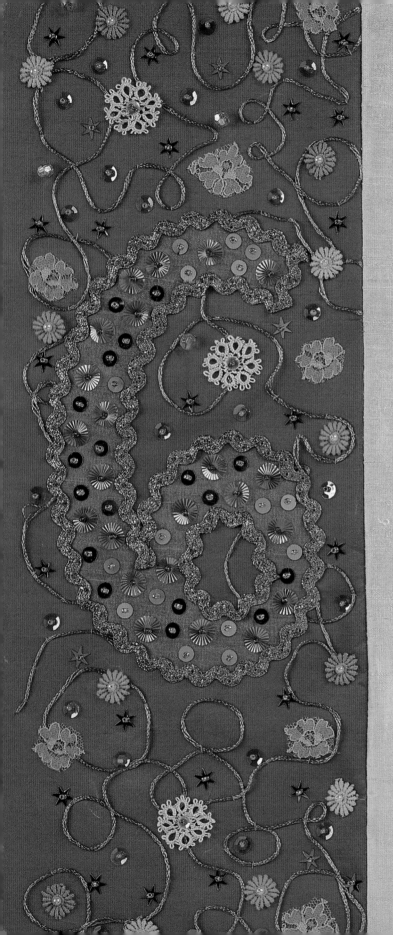

On the sixth day of Christmas
My true love gave to me

Six geese a-laying,
Five golden rings,
Four calling birds,
Three French hens,
Two turtle-doves,
And a partridge in a pear tree.

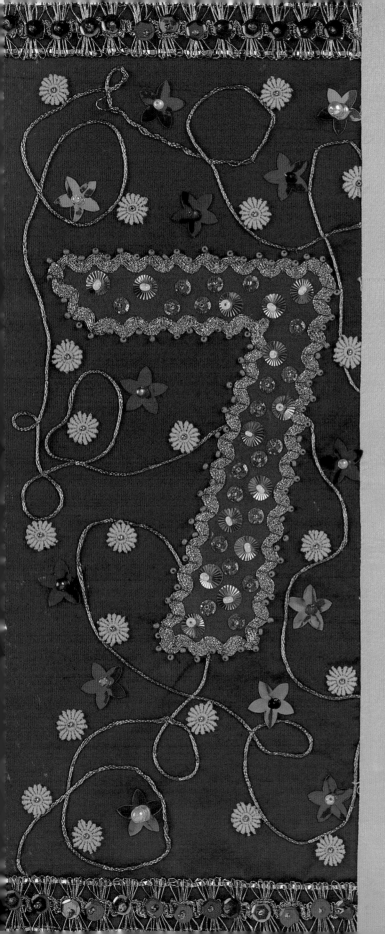

On the seventh day of Christmas
My true love gave to me

Seven swans a-swimming,

Six geese a-laying,

Five golden rings,

Four calling birds,

Three French hens,

Two turtle-doves,

And a partridge in a pear tree.

On the eighth day of Christmas
My true love gave to me

Eight maids a-milking,

Seven swans a-swimming,

Six geese a-laying,

Five golden rings,

Four calling birds,

Three French hens,

Two turtle-doves,

And a partridge in a pear tree.

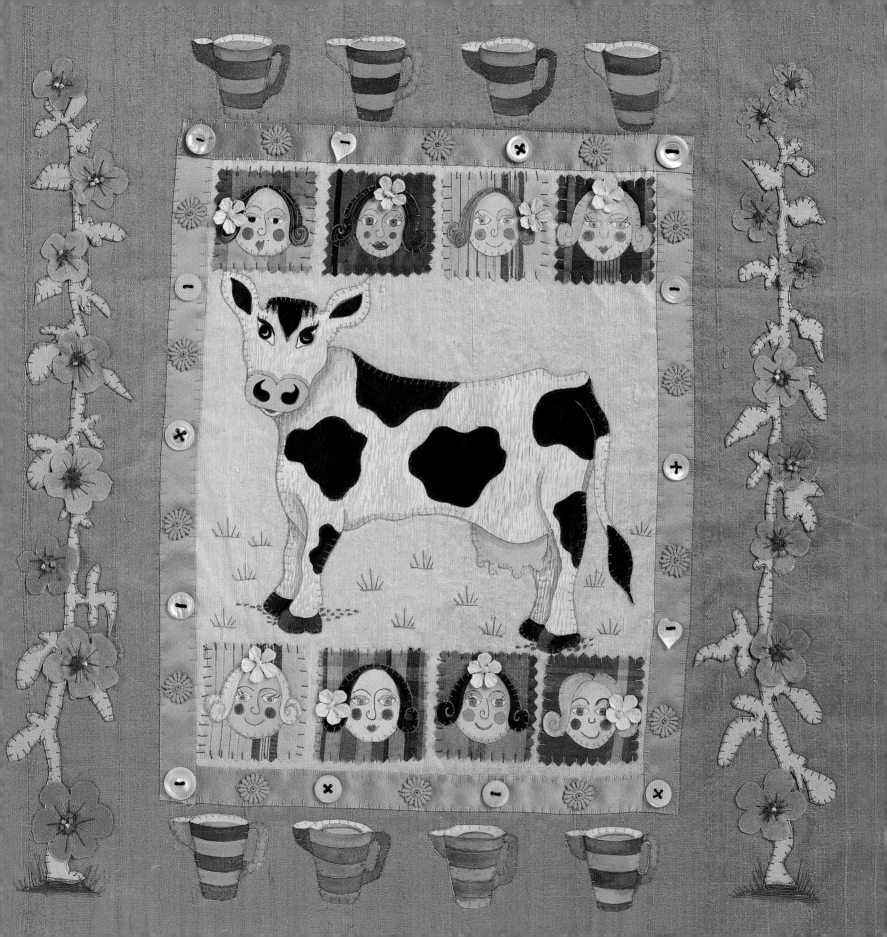

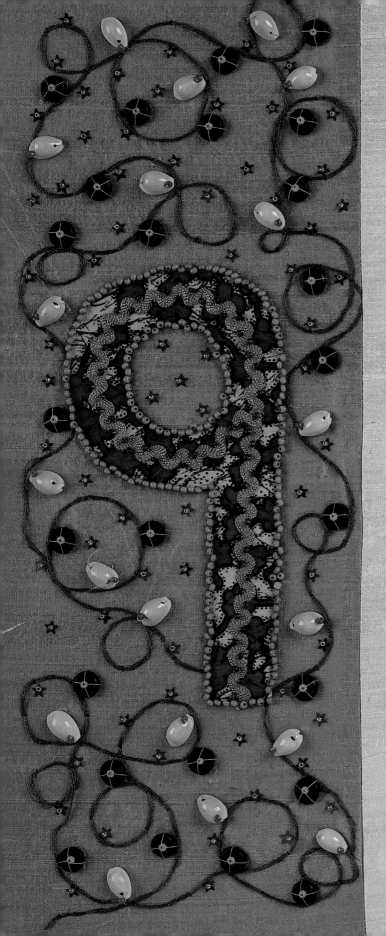

On the ninth day of Christmas
My true love gave to me

Nine drummers drumming,

Eight maids a-milking,

Seven swans a-swimming,

Six geese a-laying,

Five golden rings,

Four calling birds,

Three French hens,

Two turtle-doves,

And a partridge in a pear tree.

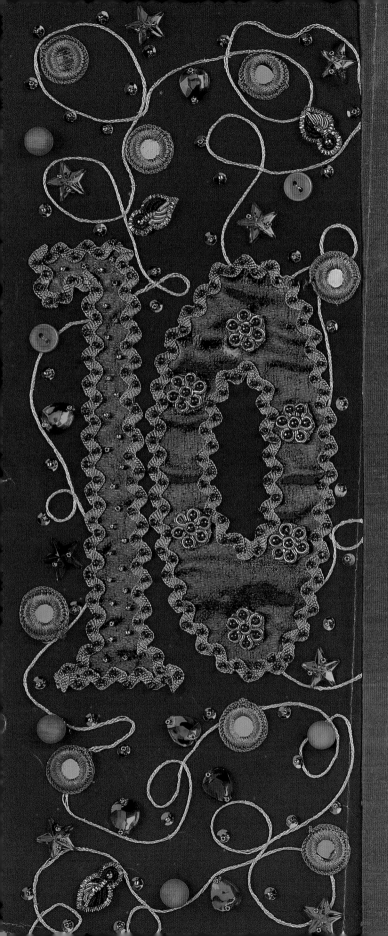

On the tenth day of Christmas
My true love gave to me

Ten pipers piping,
Nine drummers drumming,
Eight maids a-milking,
Seven swans a-swimming,
Six geese a-laying,
Five golden rings,
Four calling birds,
Three French hens,
Two turtle-doves,
And a partridge in a pear tree.

On the eleventh day of Christmas
My true love gave to me

Eleven ladies dancing,
Ten pipers piping,
Nine drummers drumming,
Eight maids a-milking,
Seven swans a-swimming,
Six geese a-laying,
Five golden rings,
Four calling birds,
Three French hens,
Two turtle-doves,
And a partridge in a pear tree.

On the twelfth day of Christmas
My true love gave to me

Twelve lords a-leaping,
Eleven ladies dancing,
Ten pipers piping,
Nine drummers drumming,
Eight maids a-milking,
Seven swans a-swimming,
Six geese a-laying,
Five golden rings,
Four calling birds,
Three French hens,
Two turtle-doves,
And a partridge in a pear tree.

Barefoot Books
Celebrating Art and Story

At Barefoot Books, we celebrate art and story with books that open the hearts and minds of children from all walks of life, inspiring them to read deeper, search further, and explore their own creative gifts. Taking our inspiration from many different cultures, we focus on themes that encourage independence of spirit, enthusiasm for learning, and acceptance of other traditions. Thoughtfully prepared by writers, artists and storytellers from all over the world, our products combine the best of the present with the best of the past to educate our children as the caretakers of tomorrow.

www.barefootbooks.com